ENJOY YOUR
GOLF

ENJOY YOUR GOLF

How to lift your game and
lower your handicap

MIKE HAMLIN

Patrick Stephens Limited

British Library Cataloguing in Publication Data

Hamlin, Mike
    Enjoy your golf.
    How to lift your game and
    lower your handicap.
    1. Golf—Manuals
    I. Title
    796.352'3

ISBN 1-85260-209-0

Patrick Stephens is part of the
Thorsons Publishing Group

Printed in Great Britain by Woolnough Bookbinding Limited,
Irthlingborough, Northamptonshire

10 9 8 7 6 5 4 3 2 1

Contents

For
Christopher Charles

Preface

I first started to play golf in November three years ago and my relatives, in the height of their annual quandary as to what to buy 'him' for Christmas, seized on this opportunity to supply me with a host of golf instruction books written by well-known professionals.

It soon became apparent to me that the majority of these books were written by experts trying to teach me, the reader, how to be an expert as well. I wanted to write to them all and tell them how optimistic I thought they were in allowing their books to become acquired by people like me. I was talked out of it.

1

At the beginning my ambition was to gain a proper handicap (I was ecstatic when the figure 28 went up alongside my name on the club noticeboard) and then (and I spent a year working at this) it was to reduce this figure to the point where I could actually

BEAT TWENTY!

2

Introduction

Most people are aware that if you reverse the letters of our favourite game you end up with a 'Flog' and that is just what it can turn out to be on a bad day.

One of Jack Nicklaus' oft quoted expressions is that 'We rarely play as well as we think we ought to', but this was small consolation to me when sometimes I couldn't believe quite how badly I had played. I never had any illusions about becoming a scratch player but felt that there must be some simple way to avoid being a total disaster all the time. Surely there must be a few basic rules that would get me to, and keep me on, the right side of twenty over par and thereby give me a chance to really get some enjoyment out of the game.

I have taken lessons from good professionals and have learned something new from each one but, as a complete novice, I noticed one inevitable assumption made by most pro's — an assumption that the average student is reasonably physically and mentally co-ordinated. Even for those of us who feel relatively confident that we are — there is nothing quite like a half-hour golf lesson to leave the matter slightly in doubt!

In the midst of my despair, my wife decided to take up the game to try to find out what was making her normally emotionally stable husband quite so neurotic. It was while watching her practise in the back garden that I realized she was a mirror image of all my problems and, like me, she was starting to get so far in the forest that she couldn't see the wood for the trees. I decided to try and formulate some basic, easy to remember rules that would hardly make us experts (I didn't and still don't have anything like the knowledge required) but would improve our game

'. . . an assumption that the average student is reasonably physically and mentally co-ordinated . . .'

and, hopefully, give us some degree of consistency.

What I have tried to do in this small booklet is to explain my conclusions as simply as possible such that when my game is in danger of falling completely apart, the recall of one or two of these rules enables me to pull things slightly more together and salvage something from the round. I apologise in advance to those purists who may insist (perhaps quite rightly in some cases) that some techniques I am going to suggest are incorrect in the pursuance of perfect golf. I would ask them to bear with me as the whole purpose of this book is not to help its readers achieve perfection but simply to BEAT TWENTY and *enjoy* their golf.

These ideas have certainly worked for us and I am confident that unless you already play on the international professional circuit there will be occasions when they can do the same for you.

4

'If you can't see it . . .'

One of the first simple demonstrations that I use if friends ask me for some advice is to place a ball on the ground in front of their putter. I then ask them to putt it gently and, naturally, they have no difficulty in doing so. I then move the ball up to 4 inches in any direction several times and each time ask them again to putt it. Again — no problem.

I then ask them to look at an imaginary pin at the end of the garden and then try and putt the ball without looking down at it. The results are totally predictable in that most of the time they miss the ball completely and, if they don't, the best they achieve is a glancing blow which sends the ball off at an angle.

We wouldn't dream of trying to hit a tennis or squash ball without looking at it yet how many times do we see someone out on the course staring steadfastly over the horizon when they are only half way through their swing.

Then we see them wondering why they haven't hit the ball properly and this brings us to the first rule of any golf shot whether it be with driver or with putter.

YOU WILL NEVER HIT THE BALL PROPERLY IF YOU DON'T LOOK AT IT

'. . . we wouldn't dream of trying to hit a tennis or squash ball without looking at it . . .'

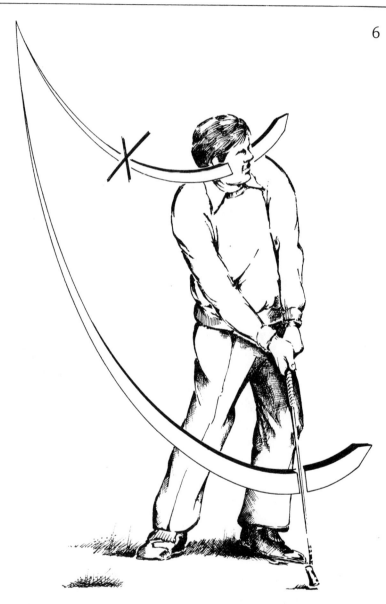

6

'. . . standing up halfway through the backswing . . .'

My head is important?

Your golf swing should pivot around your spine with your head remaining in the same place throughout the swing. Yet in how many of us is this really the case?

I usually make my second (and last!) demonstration by asking the recipient of the advice to hold a golf club with their left finger and thumb right at the top of the shaft and swing it gently like a pendulum using their wrist alone. (Diag 7a). I then ask them to gently tap a ball on the ground in front of them and, naturally, they find this quite easy as they automatically adjust the height of their wrist to ensure that the club only grazes the ground before striking the ball. As long as they keep their wrist at the same height then every one is a winner.

I now get in on the act and, as the club head is coming forward, I either lift their hand or depress it. The result is that they either miss the ball completely or hit the ground prior to impact.

I then explain that the purpose of this demonstration is to liken the position of the wrist in this gentle wrist swing to the position of the head in a normal golf swing (Diag 7b) and this brings me to another rule.

IF YOUR HEAD GOES UP AND DOWN DURING YOUR SWING, YOU HAVEN'T A HOPE OF CONSISTENTLY BRINGING THE CLUB HEAD THROUGH IN THE SAME PLACE

I first noticed this when a friend took a video of my practice swing and I was surprised (and horrified!) to see

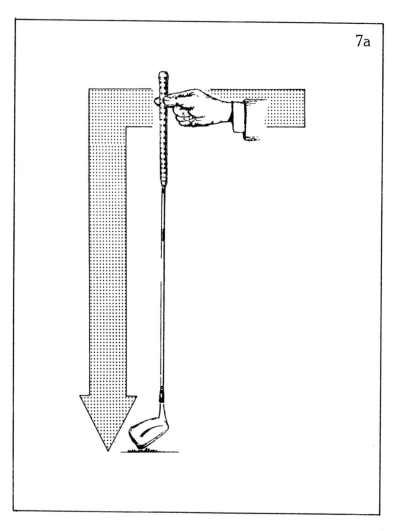

that I was standing up halfway through the backswing. Since I have consciously tried to keep my head at the same level during my swing I have noticed a marked reduction in the number of 'thinned' shots and large divots flying through the air.

7b

Getting a grip on things

*'Golf is a left-handed game played by
right-handed players'*

We have all heard that statement so many times — but
what does it mean? It took a little while for me to
understand but I found that it all begins with grip.

I never realized quite how important the grip on a golf
club is until I changed my own grip to the one
recommended by most professionals. The grip most pro's
prefer is in diagram 8a and the one that most of us start
off with if we are not careful is in diagram 8b.

The fundamental error that we all tend to make as
beginners is to try to grip the club in a manner that feels
'comfortable' to us rather than in the manner in which we
are instructed as this feels slightly odd and uncomfortable.

Every time I play golf I can see players gripping the
club firmly with their right hand and especially with the
base of their right thumb over their left thumb nail and
their right thumbnail glinting white with the effort. Their
swing often looks like a cross between a cricket cover
drive and a baseball shot out over first base, and the ball,
understandably enough, goes anywhere. This, I am afraid,
is inevitable with such a grip.

The reason one is asked to put the right hand slightly
over the left with the 'V' of the right thumb and forefinger
pointing down the shaft (Diag 8a) is because it severely inhibits
right arm (unwanted) input into the swing. Try holding
a cricket stump or large stick and hitting a plastic practice
golf ball with your right thumb gripping on top of the stick

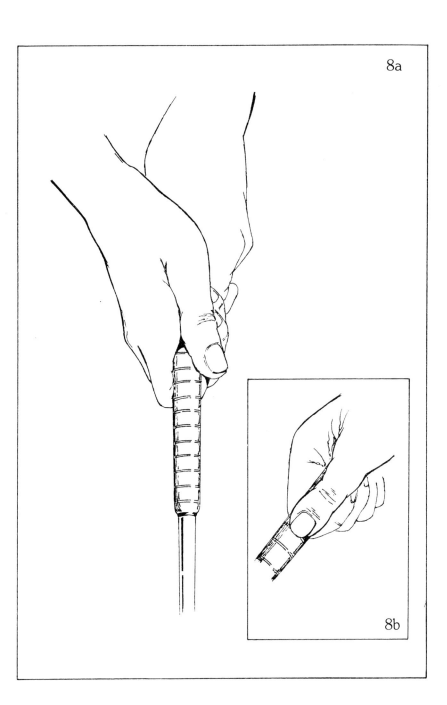

9

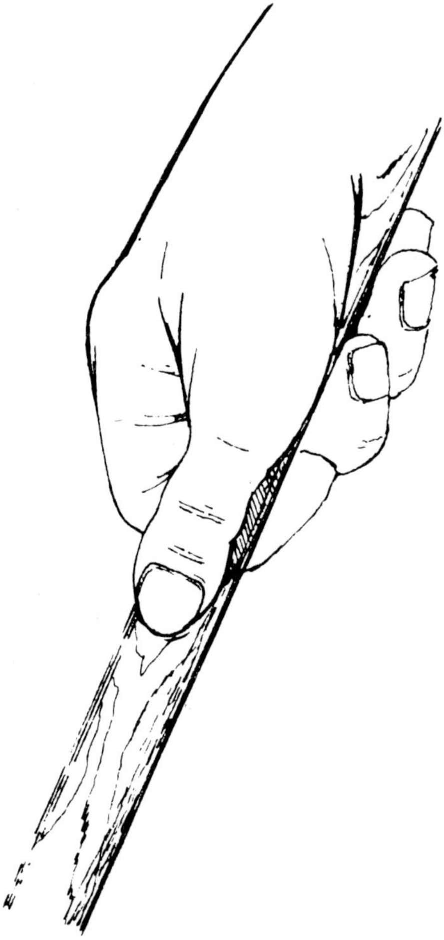

and you will find that it is easy and you have lots of control (Diag 9). Move your grip anti-clockwise around the stick and now try it with your thumb on the left hand side of your grip. It will feel 'cack-handed' and be impossible for your right arm to generate any fundamental degree of control or force.

Great — this is just what we want! So . . .

IF YOU GRIP THE CLUB IN A WAY THAT LETS YOUR RIGHT ARM EXERCISE *ANY* CONTROL — IT WILL

. . . and it follows that if your right arm does exercise any control then you can kiss goodbye any hope of a consistent or reliable swing. Therefore . . .

GRIP THE CLUB AS FIRMLY AS POSSIBLE WITH YOUR LEFT HAND AND AS GENTLY AS YOU CAN WITH YOUR RIGHT HAND

Why can't I use my right arm

For any naturally right handed person there is an almost uncontrollable desire to inject some fundamental force into the swing with the right arm. However, it is a sad fact of golfing life that to do so is a certain guarantee that you will not hit the ball anywhere near as well as you could or should.

Imagine standing in front of a tennis ball suspended from the branch of a tree in front of you. If you try and hit it quickly with a racket in your right hand you will have to either lunge at it or, at least, thrust hard forward with your right shoulder. If you hit it with a racket in your left hand the ball will fly away much quicker and this is a very important point to note. It is because you can get your left arm to move far quicker than your right arm/shoulder combination.

A golf ball puts up imperceptible resistance to a club and thus the distance that a golf ball will travel is a direct result of the speed of the club head at impact. It is *not* a product of the effort that goes into the shot.

It is a simple fact of human construction that you can get more speed (not necessarily more *power* — it is SPEED that we are looking for) into a swing with your left arm than you can with your right. Your poor right arm cannot accelerate through a swing simply because YOUR BODY IS IN THE WAY! On a left-powered swing the body follows behind.

This is possibly the most important lesson that you will have to learn in golf and you will have to learn it

'. . . blasting a daisy into oblivion while standing on
your left foot alone . . .'

eventually if you really want to improve.

Trying to be a 'right-handed' player has other disadvantages as well. For instance, try holding the club with your right hand and blasting a daisy into oblivion while standing on your left foot alone.

Now get up off the grass and try again.

After a few more attempts it soon becomes apparent that if you want to hit the ball with your RIGHT HAND then you will have to keep your weight on your RIGHT FOOT — and, oh dear, this brings us on to the next chapter.

Perils of playing off the back foot

I have a very dear friend who has perfected playing off the back foot so that it is not so much a science but more a kind of art form. His basic ability is certainly no less than mine (although he does sensitively admit to being a 'little' older). Nevertheless, he is usually a good ten strokes behind me on every round.

He just doesn't give himself a chance with his current technique and the reasons are quite simple.

1. You cannot swing through a ball with your right arm because your body is in the way.

2. Because your body is in the way, the club head will invariably come in an arc across the back of the ball from right to left and this imparts spin that will give you a comprehensive (and depressing) fade every time. (Diag 11)

3. It is almost impossible to get any club head acceleration due to right hand wrist action during the downward part of the swing. Effective wrist action comes from the left (see 'breaking the wrists' in chapter 8, 'The Swing').

The 'art form' exponent will compensate for these problems in a most ingenious way. Firstly, by taking any weight at all off his left foot, he will spin hard on the ball

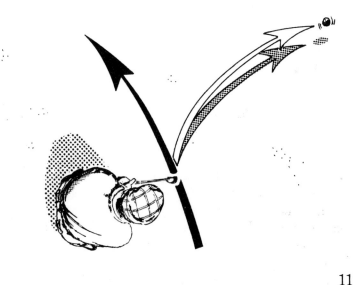

of his right foot during the swing ending up with both feet in 'line astern' pointing towards the pin. This helps to get his body out of the way.

Secondly, he will thrust hard forward with his right shoulder to 'push' the club through and thus avoid coming across the back of the ball. This technique has an unexpected result sometimes as, if he is trying to give it 'the big one' on a 400 yard plus par 4, this thrust with the right shoulder will actually take the club head across the ball in a reverse direction from left to right thus imparting a nasty hook. Having been aiming up the left hand side of the fairway to allow for his fade he now watches, with inconsolable mortification, as the ball doesn't turn gently right but arcs left to disappear out of the far left hand side of the *adjacent* fairway. (Diag 12)

The trouble is that he does hit a few shots every round

where the thrust of his shoulder from left to right balances the natural tendency of the back foot player for the club to come across the ball from right to left — and the ball actually goes in a straight line!

This encourages him to think that with just a little more care and concentration he will get it right whereas, in reality, by persisting in controlling his club with his right hand and arm he *has* to play off his back foot to avoid falling over and thus all of his 'good' shots are pure luck. Sadly he cannot possibly improve his game until he dramatically changes his technique.

His game is actually held together by exceptional body and eye co-ordination but with his current technique (or lack of!) he only needs a very slight 'off day' and his whole game disintegrates.

If only he could see himself on video.

12

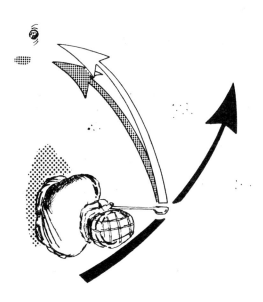

Turn your back into success

I once read one sentence of a book that led to a quantum leap in my search for improvement although for a week, until I had actually tried what it was suggesting, I wasn't sure that it would really make much difference.

It said that Tom Watson advised players to turn the back towards the pin they were aiming for as part of the overall backswing. This seemed a good deal more difficult than the 'half turn' that I had been using up until then (Diag 13) but I thought it was worth giving it a try. At that stage and time *anything* was worth a try!

The resulting improvement was amazing — and all for simple, understandable reasons.

Firstly the flatter 'half turn' that I had been using always resulted in a bit of right shoulder 'push' during my swing. However, turning my back that much further round so it was facing in the direction I wished to hit the ball made it almost impossible for my right shoulder to get in on the action.

And, as if this wasn't good enough, I also found that the greater arc that my left shoulder now had to travel through during my swing caused my left arm to 'whip' through considerably faster than it used to before — and all this with NO EXTRA EFFORT.

Suddenly I was hitting the ball further and straighter than I had ever done before.

'Tom', I thought, 'You are a hero! In one sentence you have taken five strokes off my handicap!'

The 'half turn' never quite worked . . .

The swing

The grip: We have discussed this in detail and the only extra point to add is that you must consciously *not* slacken your left hand at the top of the backswing and end up 'flopping' the club through. This is inviting the right arm to take over.

Your head: I can't say it often enough — keep your head in the same place throughout the swing and keep your eyes on the ball! Try practising a few swings with a book balanced on your head and if it stays there until you are well into your follow through then you know you are in good shape.

Your back: Turn your back towards the pin.

The left arm: KEEP IT STRAIGHT! The moment that you bend your left arm you substantially reduce the chances of the club passing back through the position that you have just raised it from. Also, as your swing progresses down, the club will start driving your arm straight against the elbow joint. This will give you a very, very sore elbow in no time at all (and I speak from tender experience).

The backswing: Move the club SLOWLY backwards, thinking about what you are going to do, and in your early stages of learning, do not raise your left arm above the horizontal. When you are as good as Ballesteros you can but, until then, there is no need to and it won't help, as it is very unlikely that you will be able to keep control of the club off an exaggerated backswing. Take your time. Flicking it quickly back and then forwards will never give you a chance to keep control of things.

The wrists: 'Let your wrists break gently as the club head approaches the ball'. That's what my first instructor told me and I thought he was being sarcastic! What he was actually trying to tell me was that if I cocked my wrists slightly at the top of the backswing then they should straighten naturally as my swing progressed and thus accelerate the club head as it approached the ball.

The start down: Initiate the first downward movement of the club with *left arm only* and remember — DON'T TRY TOO HARD!

The *harder* you try, the more you 'stiffen' up and the SLOWER goes your swing.

There is a finite limit to how much impetus you can impart with your left arm alone and, if you try to exceed this, your body has nowhere else to go for extra power except to ask your right arm for help.

At this point you will be moving back to square one (as we have discussed before) in that the moment your right arm exercises *any* positive input into your swing then as a reliable and consistent action — your swing is effectively finished!

The follow through: The importance of a full follow through is often under-estimated and a short, restricted follow through is often a good indication that you are trying to 'hit' the ball rather than swing through it. Trying to consciously hit the ball will simply tense the muscles just before impact and REDUCE the speed of your club head. This is the last thing that we want, so just keep the club flowing through the ball and up in the direction of the pin.

There is so much to any game (especially golf!) that it sometimes seems impossible to remember all the points of technique that one should. One might ask whether it is possible to condense all of these points into a small, easily remembered package. Well I think I have to say that, sadly, I don't think that it is

BUT

if I were to recommend three things only to remember that would give your swing greater control and consistency — they would be as follows:

1. **Left arm/grip:** Straight arm, tight grip.

2. **Head:** Do not move until after the ball is struck.

3. **Back:** Turn your back to the pin.

Putting it all together

Let's pick up the club and see how what we have read in the previous pages applies to real life. The club will feel a little odd if you have been holding it incorrectly up until now but try a few gentle swings with no ball (preferably in an area of the garden that isn't too important) and see how this feels.

At this point I suggest you try to decapitate a few daisies at the back of the lawn. The daisies will give you something to aim at, so you can see where the club head is coming through, but there is no ball there to get the adrenalin running. This helps swinging through the ball rather than trying to hit it.

Ever noticed how the professionals end up with a flourishing follow through? (Well, everyone except Arnold Palmer perhaps.) If you try to emulate them just a little you will find that it actually helps you position the club during your backswing.

Try a dozen practice swings using hardly any backswing at all but a full follow through. Then *stay relaxed*, don't try too hard, and try a normal backswing keeping the follow through going.

Feels better doesn't it?

One of the major unsung benefits of a full follow through is that it forces you to transfer your weight onto your left foot and simply playing off the front foot will eliminate a vast proportion of your hooks and slices (see 'Perils of Playing Off The Back Foot').

This is in addition to the fact that if you do try a full

follow through with your weight on your right foot you run the risk of sitting down sharply with an unceremonious 'plonk'.

I'm so sorry sir but we do have a waiting list

In retrospect, one of the best things that happened to me, on having decided to take up golf, was that it was temporarily impossible to get membership into any club. So, after a few lessons, this forced me to try my hand at the local 'par three' course.

What a learning process that was!

Little greens surrounded by little bunkers at the end of 100-130 yard fairways: short, but highly accurate, approach shots became the norm, rather than the exception, as without them you just wouldn't score at all.

The benefits of having developed a good short game proved immeasurable when I finally got around to playing on a real golf course — especially when I started to play with some other 28 handicappers who had only ever played on a full-size course.

They could certainly hit the ball further than I could but when it came to the final approach shot to the green (especially from under 50 yards) I used to see some of the most ingenious and creative golf shots that you could possibly imagine! There were snatched 3 irons along with putted and poked 8 irons and even a putter off a half back swing.

I found all of these shots very hard to believe as without too much fuss I used to pull out a wedge and,

"Ah! I see young Raymond is using his *wedge* again."

with vintage par three technique, 'plop' there it was on the green.

On asking my new friends why they didn't use a wedge there was a collective intake of breath through clenched teeth and the general answer was that it was 'far too dangerous'. Either the divot would go further than the ball or (worse still!) the shot would be 'thinned' and the ball would set off like a bionic torpedo passing two inches above the green at about 90 knots to disappear in the nettles out on the far side.

After a few rounds I realized the tremendous advantage I had inadvertently acquired by playing 'par three' golf for six months. Unless you put your tee shot on the green on our local par three then your second shot was always a wedge or a sand iron! There was simply no other club to sensibly use and so I had been forced into learning how to use it, if not properly, then certainly effectively.

There is no magic technique to mastering your wedge and sand iron but just a little regular practice in the garden with a plastic ball will give you a lot of extra confidence. Remember to keep it A LEFT ARM SHOT and to resist the temptation to 'poke' at it and try to shovel it up with a right arm/hand combination as this will invariably result in a 'thinned' shot. Don't try to 'nip' the ball off the surface. Aim to hit firmly into the ground just short of the ball and you will be surprised how well this works.

Never try to hit a gentle, measured shot as this will give you a guaranteed 'thin'. If it is a shorter distance then hold the club further down the shaft and play the same full stroke. You can vary the distance more confidently by moving your hands up and down the shaft rather than trying to play strong and weak shots.

Nowadays my fairway game comes and goes like everyone else's but my short game is always there and on

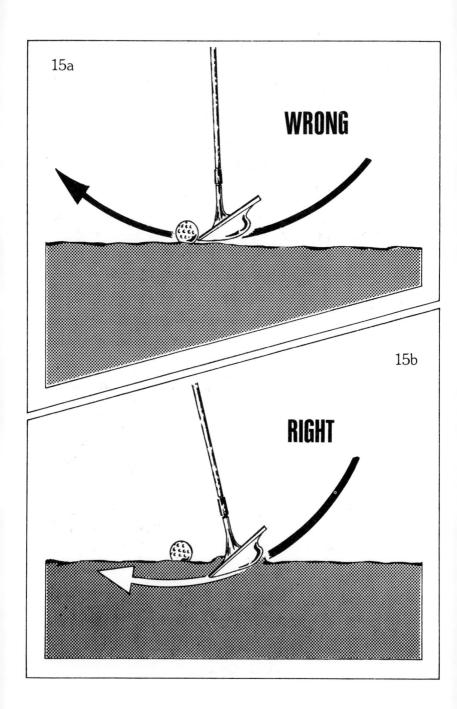

15a **WRONG**

15b **RIGHT**

every round I play it gets me out of trouble. It doesn't matter whether I miss-hit my drive or a disappointing second shot is 10 to 50 yards short of the green — my third will invariably give me a putt. It even works on the 'agony' shot where, in the height of summer, you have to play off a piece of 'brown concrete' two feet short of a bunker to a pin ten feet the other side. With two putts this means I can nearly always salvage a 5 on a par 4 hole even when I haven't started it too well.

So what is the message in all this? Well it is probably one of the most important lessons that I have learned in the limited time that I have been playing golf.

PRACTISE, PRACTISE, PRACTISE UNTIL YOU HAVE DEVELOPED A LOVE AFFAIR WITH YOUR PITCHING WEDGE AND SAND IRON

They will get you out of all kinds of trouble every time you play.

Oh no! where's that one going?

'The fairway unravelled before his relentless gaze. A mere suspicion of a smile passed fleetingly across his granite features as, without moving his steely grey eyes from the objective, he reached, unlooking, for his driver.

His partners fell back in a hush from the tee as with ultimate care and deliberation he placed that small plastic peg in the ground. As the great man had his back to us we shall never know whether it was with love or with sympathy that he finally positioned his ball on the tee. He shuffled gently assuming a poise reminiscent of a mamba coiled to strike before slowly raising the club ever further and higher behind him. He paused momentarily before, with eyes bulging, he commenced the downward movement of his club'. . . thereby unleashing a chain of events totally beyond his control!

Not the least of which was ultimately trying to find his wretched ball!

I used to have terrible trouble off the tee even when I seemed to be doing OK with woods off the fairway and, as you can imagine, it all turned out to be too much adrenalin. When the ball is on the fairway you have to think carefully and keep your swing well under control otherwise the shot is a total disaster. However, when I came to the tee I just couldn't resist the overwhelming macho desire to 'give it one' — with equally predictable results.

It took a lot of mental control to overcome this as it only took one extra long drive to be more than enough

". . . thereby unleashing a chain of events totally beyond his control . . ."

encouragement for me to give it everything at the next few tees. The penny finally dropped when I found myself being regularly beaten by someone who didn't have a wood in their bag. They just used to pop a 3 iron 180-190 yards right up the middle every time.

It is surprising how little — if anything — you actually do lose in terms of distance if you reduce the amount of *effort* that goes into your drive and you bring it more under control. This really is the important lesson to learn here.

GO FOR ACCURACY NOT DISTANCE FROM THE TEE

Far better to be 200 yards up the middle than 250 yards into the middle of nowhere.

My own speciality when 'overcooking' it off the tee, having run out of available power with my left arm is to push my right shoulder through during the swing down. With me this moves the club head slightly out on its arc so that only the edge of the heel of the club makes contact. So, after a mighty grunt, heave, effort and swish the ball scuttles off sharp left for about 30 yards and generally doesn't even make the fairway proper.

Of my two playing partners, one has developed a near carbon copy of my trick, whereas the other leans back and whilst gripping the club firmly with his right hand executes a mighty cover drive out onto the adjacent fairway.

We all then look at each other, put another ball on the tee and go back to doing it properly.

Why does it all go wrong when I try to hit it a long way?

One of the biggest problems I had once was that whenever I tried to hit a long shot from the fairway — not a lot happened!

I was very happy swatting the ball with confidence (and a fair degree of accuracy) with my 8 iron but when I tried to use my 3 or 4 iron I couldn't seem to get it any further and usually not even as far.

One of the reasons was a total confidence failure in that as soon as I picked up a long iron I was consumed with the depressing thought 'Oh no, I never hit it properly with one of these,' but I only felt like this because I was failing all the time. The important question was — why was I failing all the time?

Firstly I considered why the ball should travel further after being struck with a 3 iron, as opposed to an 8 iron, and the first reason is easy to see in that the club head is angled differently and thus a 3 iron sends the ball out on a lower trajectory. The second reason is just as important and it lies in the length of the shaft. Just by having a shaft approximately 10 per cent longer than an 8 iron then, off an identical swing, the 3 iron club head will travel 10 per cent faster and this alone will impart substantially more energy into the ball.

So, why wasn't my 3 iron sending the ball substantially further than my 8 iron?

The answer, not surprisingly, was in my brain. The reason that I didn't have a problem with my 8 iron was because I did not intend or expect the ball to go that far so I was always relaxed. However, when I picked up a long iron I would look at the distance and my subconscious would mutter to me 'You had better give this one a bit of a thwack or it will never get there'. The consequence of this was that I would try to hit the ball too hard and make pretty well every mistake that we have discussed so far. What was happening was that I was being 'psyched out' by the apparently huge distance I was hoping the ball would go.

I have overcome this problem by simple self deception.

Now, whenever I am in a position where a good long iron shot is needed, I briefly assess the distance and then pick the club. Without looking up the fairway any more I try a few practice swings (honestly my practice swings are the most beautiful, flowing balanced affairs known to man — as long as there isn't a ball around!). Finally with one quick look up the fairway to check that I am pointing in the right direction, I address the ball and, even though I may be holding a 3 iron, keep the following though firmly in the front of my mind:

THIS IS GOING TO BE A RELAXED 8 IRON AND I AM GOOD AT THEM

The very first time I tried this technique (and most subsequent times as well) the ball screamed off up the fairway and, after a good drive, put me on a 400 yard par 4 green in two shots.

I have never seen my good friend and playing partner look so depressed!

Well I'll be bunkered!

'"A good firm one up the middle and I'm there", he thought. So with club head having moved swiftly in a fluid arc the ball flew up the fairway . . . only to fade minutely in the last 25% of its flight ("It was the wind, it was definitely the wind!") and bounce gently into the bunker on the right hand side of the green.

'It was one of the best drives he had done this year and he had followed it with a beautifully middled 4 iron so the ball flew, nay it soared, up towards the pin. For the next few moments he was on an all time high but in the few seconds it took to fade, drop and bounce into the bunker he was emotionally transformed from a "conqueror of men" to a "balloon with a hole in it".'

We've all been there haven't we?

Isn't it amazing the depths of the depression we can sink into just by seeing our ball nestling gently in the sand. Psychologically I used to have exactly the same problem with sand shots as I did with long irons and I would have to stride manfully into the bunker whilst inwardly feeling the strength and confidence of a newly made blancmange.

As you can imagine I found the key to success in the sand is, yet again, a function of the brain as much as of the body and also, surprisingly, a function of the club as well. Whereas all of the other iron clubs from 1 to 9 have a base angle that is more or less flat, the pitching wedge is angled slightly upward and the sand iron even more so (Diag 18). The effect of this is to tend to deflect the club

'. . . the failure complex . . .'

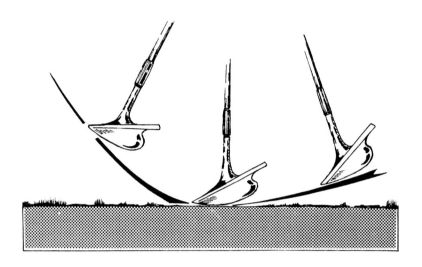

head up whenever it makes contact with the ground and I found that this was what was ruining most of my attempts to escape from the bunkers.

The average club golfer rarely acquires the wrist strength or technique to take out a divot on each iron shot in order to impart back spin to the ball. His best hope is just to scrape the grass level with the soil and make good contact. This *inability to contemplate hitting into the ground* was what gave me the greatest problem in the sand and created my 'failure complex' when my ball went into a bunker.

When I tried my standard swing at a ball nestling in the sand, my club head grazed the sand just as if it were

'. . . return to rest within a few inches of where it had started . . .'

grazing the grass, giving me a classic 'thin'. The ball would either scream off across the green to give me another challenge out of the bunker on the other side or, alternatively, hit the lip of the one I was attempting to play out of and return to rest within a few inches of where it had started. This would happen for two or three conscientious and carefully considered strokes until I got really cross and gave the ball a real welt!

Out it came in a spray of sand with no problem at all. The trouble was that I had probably been 16 over par after 15 holes and looking good but now, with 3 shots to clear the bunker, I was 19 over after 16 and my chances of beating twenty were gone.

The question was 'Why could I only succeed with sand shots when I was cross?'

Eventually the penny dropped: when I got annoyed and 'went for it' I succeeded because of the extra force behind the shot and this worked for two reasons. Firstly, it pushed the club head further into the sand before the angle of the base of the club head started to deflect up and this enabled me to get the club under the ball. Secondly, as I was now lifting out of the bunker not only the golf ball but at least its own weight in sand, the extra force carried the ball some way towards the pin. This more positive approach also cured my 'half successes' where I hadn't stopped to think that the club head was going to lift at least double the normal ball weight and although I would escape the bunker I would drop the ball on the edge of the green with a 30-foot putt still to go.

How do you quantify the extra force needed as, if you try too hard, you end up worse off than you were before?

Well, when I am in a bunker now, I visualize the pin as being at least 100 per cent further away than it really is and find that for me the extra strength that I put into the shot to reach my imaginary pin nicely compensates for

'. . . the sand traps do not now hold the terrors for me that they used to . . .'

the loss of momentum of the club head when it starts to scoop up the sand. I also have to remember to grip the club very firmly with my left hand as my swing begins and tighten my right hand for extra support against the resistance of the sand as the club approaches it. Initially I found this difficult for as soon as I tightened my right hand — my right arm took over and I ended up 'poking the fire' and stabbing at it.

However, after a little time and thought, I got the compromise right and although I certainly wouldn't describe myself as a 'bunker king' the sand traps do not now hold the terrors for me that they used to.

And after all that I four putted!

I remember vividly the first time I ever managed to get on the edge of a 400 yard par 4 green in two shots and yet still had to write a six on my scorecard. The pain lingers on!

Whilst our driving and iron play will have good days and bad days there really is no excuse for not being reasonably consistent with the putter. It requires less physical effort than any other club and so there SHOULD be less margin for error. So, why do we end up spraying the ball all over the green on some days?

Well, I have found one factor that has dramatically improved my putting and it takes us right back to the first chapter of the book.

First of all I stand back and carefully measure the amount of 'borrow' that I will have to allow for the slope. Then I address the ball and slowly look several times at the pin and the ball. This commits to memory the distance and thus the power that will be needed for this putt. When I am quite sure I have assessed this correctly *and* that my putter blade is pointing in exactly the right direction — I FIX MY EYES TOTALLY ON THE BALL!

I do not take my eyes off the ball until I have struck it and I fight to resist the enormous temptation to look up during the putt in order to see where the ball is going to go. Experience has taught me that the moment I look up and take my eyes off the ball — I won't hit it properly. If I suddenly find myself 'clacking' a few putts then I know it is because I have looked up, my shoulders have moved and I have hit the ball with the toe or heel of the putter. This, needless to say, gives the ball the wrong direction and the wrong velocity.

Try this technique yourself and remember it is very important to trust your memory regarding distance and just look at the ball until you have hit it.

As a result of this I nearly always hit the ball cleanly and it never fails to surprise me how accurately my memory records the distance and hence the power required. It all adds up towards the main objective which is to try and two putt every green. If the first putt is good then you should only be left with a tap in on the second (mind you I have known the odd 'tap in' that has made my shoelaces vibrate a bit!)

In general terms many experts far more experienced and capable than me have written lengthy tomes on how to achieve putting perfection with hints ranging from the grip of the putter to the nap of the grass. I would not presume to add to these save for two points that I think are very important for the day-to-day club golfer.

The first one is to always check the dew cover or dampness of a green before you putt. On an average British morning all the greens will be covered in dew at eight o'clock. By 10.30 am the sheltered greens will still be wet but the ones out in the open will most probably be dry and by 11.30 am they will all be dry. It is very easy to assume that, on a sheltered green, having just left a 20-foot putt six feet short that the greens are 'slow' today and we are going to have to clonk the ball a bit harder for the rest of the round. If the next green is out in the open then your next putt may well shoot ten feet past the hole and all this will do is severely erode your confidence for the rest of the round.

"It was old Jeremy's last wish — to become a part of the bunker he'd spent so much of his life in."

The second point is how much to allow for the slope of the green such that your ball curves gently into the hole. Here the important thing to remember is that you only have to allow half as much 'borrow' when putting UP a sideways slope as opposed to putting down it.

A BALL STRUCK FIRMLY UP A SLOPE WILL TURN A LOT LESS THAN ONE TAPPED DOWN IT.

Try a few practice putts from opposite sides (uphill and downhill) of a hole on a sloping green and check out the difference for yourself. Once I had discovered this difference it explained why some of my putts turned far more than I expected while others didn't seem to turn much at all.

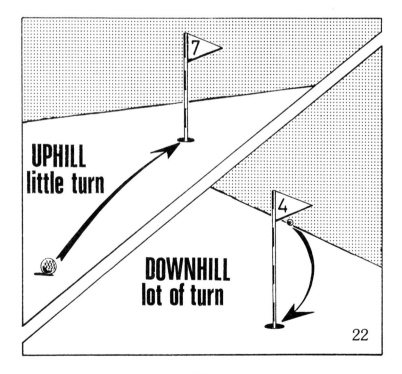

With a little help from our friends

If we could remember everything that we had been taught or had read then we would all be playing off scratch and our handicap would be a thing of the past. Sadly this is not the case, especially for me, as my brain seems to have limited memory capability regarding golf and as fast as I learn new information I tend to comprehensively forget the old!

This is where a helpful friend can be of great value with a little observation of you in action.

You may THINK that you were watching the ball when you putted.

You may THINK that you are following through with your driver.

You may THINK that you have kept your head still.

In reality an observer may point out that this is not actually the case.

I often found this when I sunk into a situation whereby it was all going wrong and yet I was sure that I was doing exactly the same as last week when it all went right.

The answer to this problem was that actually I WASN'T DOING IT EXACTLY THE SAME AS LAST WEEK — I was doing something slightly differently — and this is where an observant playing friend can be of enormous help.

'. . . on the receiving end of a self-opinionated
monologue . . .'

Mind you, asking for a little help from a playing partner is a high-risk occupation as you run the chance of ending up on the receiving end of a self-opinionated monologue every time you pick up a club. But, even if you do, pick the helpful bits out and you will be surprised how much it improves your golf.

What's going to go wrong today?

Sometimes my driver and woods would work, sometimes my long irons would work and sometimes my short irons would work but I could never seem to get them all together on the same day.

It was infuriating and for months I couldn't find the reason until eventually I discovered that I had inadvertantly developed three different swings. On further contemplation I realized that the reason I was not comfortable with, and thus rarely used my 7 iron, was probably because it fell in between two of my 'techniques'. Surprisingly it wasn't too difficult to standardize on one swing and since then things have definitely improved.

If you think that you may have the same problem then get a friend to watch you practising your swing with a 3 wood, a 3 iron and a 9 iron. If he says that they all look rather different then you may have to go back to first principles and decide which one you are going to stick with and work on.

One plus another one equals six!

One thing I have learned through depressing experience is that if I do one bad shot on an average par four and then have the misfortune to follow it without another — the best I can hope to score is a six!

Whilst we all have some days when the ball doesn't run for us, if we are honest then the majority of our dropped shots are, without doubt, 'self inflicted pain'. One of my dear departed grandmother's favourite expressions was 'Never say IF ONLY, always say NEXT TIME!' and I can't help remembering this every time I look back on one of my rounds.

'If only I hadn't used the driver on that narrow fairway, if only I hadn't tried to get out of that rough with a 5 iron, if only, if only . . .!'

I often used to drop shots not by attempting ones that were beyond my capability but by attempting some that were beyond anyone's capability! If I can just get it from over here to over there in one then I've a chance of getting level with him! What a recipe for disaster that always turned out to be.

If you are up against a very steep-faced bunker then come out backwards or sideways. If there is a tree in the way — go round it. If you are in the rough then just get it safely back on the fairway — don't go for distance! It is probably the rough that gives us most of our challenges

'. . . if it's risky with one
shot but safe with two . . .'

on the average club course and I'm sure that the stuff around the edge of our local course is cut to make ropes for ocean-going liners!

The current expression is 'percentage golf' but what does this mean? In short — if its risky with one shot but safe with two — take two!

The simple adoption of a 'percentage mentality' now saves me several shots on every round.

Conclusion

Well that's it! Keeping some of the aforementioned in my mind some of the time has helped me claw my handicap down to 12 and I think that I'm about due for another reduction any time now. I also think I have finally learned that golf is a game where success, for the most part, is inversely proportional to effort.

Mind you, in the midst of our quest to improve our golf and enjoy it more, the one thing I haven't mentioned, and it is desperately important, is the need to concentrate; THINK, just a little, before every shot. Think not only HOW to hit the ball but WHERE to hit it. For instance, if the pin is on the edge of the green don't aim for it but aim for the middle of the green. That means that even with a little fade or draw on the shot your next club will still be a putter.

It is difficult to establish a balance between enjoyment and concentration and, indeed, one of my friends has confessed that the moment he really starts to enjoy himself it all goes wrong. Another of my friends confirmed that this went for other aspects of his social life as well. So it would appear that golf is a microcosm of life's problems as a whole . . .

. . . but we love it don't we?

"Concentrate on your game . . ."